VELAZQUEZ

Biographies by
ELIZABETH RIPLEY

BOTTICELLI
DURER
GAINSBOROUGH
PICASSO
RAPHAEL
TITIAN
WINSLOW HOMER
LEONARDO DA VINCI
MICHELANGELO
REMBRANDT
RUBENS
GOYA
VAN GOGH

VELAZQUEZ

A Biography by
ELIZABETH RIPLEY

J. B. LIPPINCOTT COMPANY
Philadelphia   New York

ILLUSTRATIONS

ON THE SIXTH OF JUNE, 1599, THE SON of Juan Rodriguez de Silva and Geronima Velazquez was baptized in the Church of San Pedro in Seville. According to the Spanish custom the child was named for both his parents.

Diego Rodriguez de Silva y Velazquez was a quiet child whose big dark eyes seemed to take in everything he saw. His parents, who were respected citizens of Seville, could afford to give their son an education. Diego soon learned to read and write and to speak several languages. He was a good-natured, friendly boy, but he preferred to be alone. Sometimes he lingered on his way to school watching the people in the marketplace. He was fascinated by the dark-skinned Moors in turbans, the weather-beaten sailors, and the sturdy peasants tending their booths piled high with vegetables, fish, and fruits. Sometimes he made sketches of these people in the margins of his schoolbooks.

When Diego was eleven, he told his father that he wanted to be an artist. His parents were delighted, for there were many artists in Seville who made a good living by their painting. They consulted Pacheco, a cultivated gentleman who painted stilted religious pictures for many Spanish churches. Pacheco agreed to give Diego bed, board, and clothing and teach him the craft of painting.

The master was impressed by his talented young pupil and his admiration of Diego grew each year. He hoped the boy would become a painter of religious subjects as there were many orders to be filled for churches in Seville. But saints and Madonnas did not interest Velazquez. He wanted to paint the men and women of Seville. He wandered through the narrow, crowded streets studying the different kinds of people. He stepped into cool, dark taverns where men were eating, and drinking wine. He took in every detail of these scenes, so that he could paint them later in his studio. One of his pictures showed a servant girl leaning over a kitchen table. A hard bright light coming from the left illuminated the objects on the table, so that each bowl, jug, and pitcher became a little separate still life painting.

THE SERVANT

About 1618 (21 7/8″ x 41 1/8″)
Art Institute of Chicago
Robert A. Waller Fund

Diego hired a dark-haired peasant boy to pose. He painted him "crying, laughing, without shirking any difficulty," wrote Pacheco. The boy appeared in many of Velazquez' kitchen scenes. Holding a gourd and a bottle of wine, he watched an old woman cooking eggs. On a table in the foreground Velazquez had arranged the jugs, plates, and pots he had pictured many times. Following his master's rules for painting he worked on each part with such care that the woman's firm profile and strong hands, the boy's pensive face, and the objects on the table were perfect studies in themselves.

Pictures of people eating and drinking were popular in Velazquez' day, although many artists thought the subjects too common to be called works of art. Pacheco, however, admired Diego's carefully painted kitchen and tavern scenes, or *bodegones* as they were called.

"Should not *bodegones* be esteemed?" he wrote. "Indeed, yes, if they are done as Velazquez paints them." So truthfully had his pupil represented nature that "he inspired the minds of many by his fine example."

Pacheco had grown fond of this promising young artist who had been working in his studio for eight years.

"Induced by his youth, integrity, and good qualities," wrote Pacheco, he decided Diego should marry his daughter. In the spring of 1618, pretty Juana Pacheco was married to her father's pupil. Many well-known poets and artists were invited to the wedding and were impressed by the talented but modest bridegroom.

As soon as the couple was settled in the house Pacheco gave them, Diego de Silva y Velazquez, now nineteen, opened a workshop of his own.

OLD WOMAN COOKING EGGS
1618—20 (39″ x 46″)
National Gallery of Scotland, Edinburgh

Soon after Velazquez was settled in his workshop he was commissioned to paint a religious picture for a monastery in Seville. The subject, chosen by the monks, was the "Adoration of the Kings." Following his master's rigid rules of composition for this subject, he placed the Holy Family at the entrance of a cave. Two kings kneeled with their gifts before the Christ Child, while the third, a dark-skinned Moor, stood behind them. A bright light coming from the left cast strong, clear-cut shadows which made the figures look like sculptured forms. Unlike Pacheco's lifeless figures dressed in elaborate costumes, Velazquez' models were real men and women dressed in plain clothing worn by citizens of Seville, and the gifts presented to the Christ Child were the type made by Sevillian craftsmen.

The Moorish king was dressed in black with a red cape draped across one shoulder. His dark face contrasted with the brilliant white collar at his neck. The young king kneeling in the foreground wore a brown cloak over a blue-green robe. He looked up at the baby sitting straight and alert on his mother's knee. The model for this doll-like child could have been Francesca, Velazquez' little daughter who had just been born.

The mother, whose strong hands held the child firmly on her knee, could have been a Sevillian peasant. She wore a dark cloak over a rose-colored dress, and a white cloth was draped about her head. The boy peering over the shoulder of the Moorish king looked like the one in the picture of the old woman cooking eggs.

Pacheco was impressed by the careful workmanship in Velazquez' painting. How sharply the artist had modeled the faces, hands, and drapery, yet the plastic figures looked alive. He was sure that the painting would bring more orders to Diego's workshop.

Soon after the "Adoration of the Kings" was finished, Velazquez decided to hire an apprentice to help him with his work.

ADORATION OF THE KINGS
1619 (80 1/4″ x 49 1/4″)
Prado, Madrid

While Velazquez filled commissions for religious pictures, he still found time to work on scenes taken from real life. When he walked about the city he found new subjects for *bodegones*. He decided to paint an old Corsican water-seller who was well known to the citizens of Seville. All during the summer months when water was a luxury, El Corso stood on a busy street corner, his earthenware jug beside him, dispensing cool water by the glass.

El Corso, wearing a torn brown cloak over a spotless white shirt, posed for Velazquez several times. The hard studio light coming from the left shone on the old man's bronzed, wrinkled face, his white sleeve and the perspiring jug beside him. A peasant boy, head bent forward, took the goblet from El Corso's hand. Another youth standing in the background, was drinking from a metal cup.

Pacheco, impressed by this striking likeness to El Corso, was anxious for his son-in-law to try his hand at portraits. He commissioned Diego to paint a portrait of his friend Gongora, a well-known poet who was living in Madrid. Diego was delighted, for he was anxious to see the city he had heard so much about, and to visit the Escorial which Pacheco had described. This monastery, church, and Royal Palace, built on the slopes outside Madrid, was filled with paintings by great Venetian masters.

Another of Pacheco's friends, Fonseca, a connoisseur of art, invited Diego to visit him in Madrid. Fonseca was chaplain to young King Philip IV, and offered to introduce the artist to the court.

In April, 1622, Velazquez, hopeful that he might receive a commission from the king, set off by horseback to Madrid. As he rode northwards he thought of the sunny flowering city he had left behind him. Early in May he arrived in the cold gray capital of Spain.

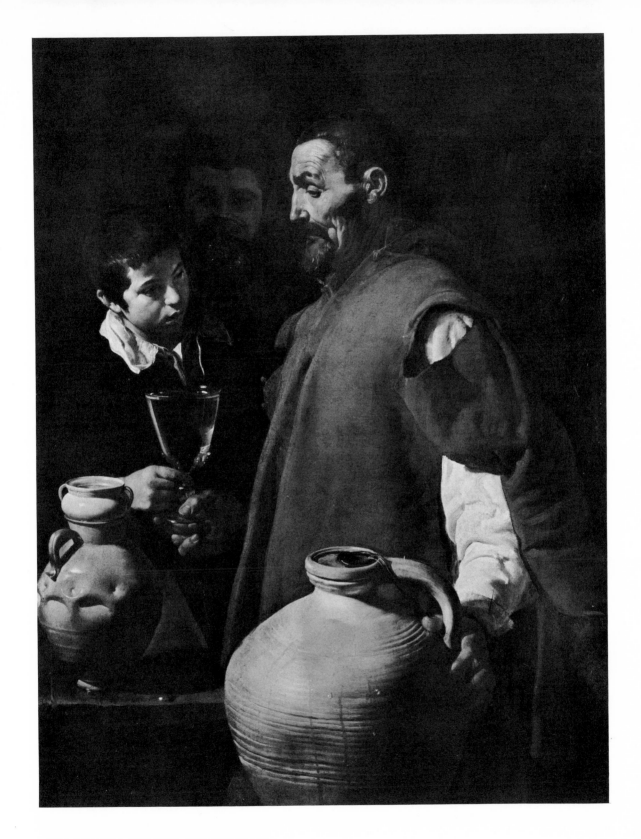

THE WATER-SELLER OF SEVILLE
1619 (41 3/8″ x 31 1/2″)
Apsley House, London
Collection of the Duke of Wellington

A piercing wind blowing across the snow-capped mountains to the north made Diego shiver as he rode through dusty streets on his way to Fonseca's house; but he was soon warmed by the welcome given him by his host. There he met many artists, writers, and musicians who had known Pacheco in Seville.

Soon after he arrived Diego visited the Escorial and walked for hours through the vast halls filled with paintings by the great Italian masters. He studied the free brush strokes used by the Venetian artist Titian, admiring the shimmering textures which were so lively compared to Pacheco's dull, smooth surfaces.

Velazquez worked for many weeks on the portrait of Gongora, carefully following the rules described in his master's book on portrait painting. The poet's stern face stood out sharply against a gray-green background. A bright light coming from the right modelled the contours of his ear, bald head, and long thin nose. A narrow white collar relieved the severity of his black priest's robe.

Velazquez listened modestly while artists and courtiers praised the portrait. How brilliantly the young Sevillian painter had captured the expression of Gongora's penetrating eyes and firm, thin mouth.

Velazquez did not wait to receive a commission from the court. Now that his mission for Pacheco was accomplished he decided to return to his family in Seville.

LUIS DE GONGORA
1622 (19 3/4″ x 15 3/4″)
Museum of Fine Arts, Boston

Soon after Velazquez' return to Seville, the nuns of San Antonio commissioned a picture for their convent. The subject, a favorite one in Spain, was the legend of St. Ildefonso. St. Ildefonso was a Spanish bishop who had a vision of the Virgin, surrounded by angels seated before the altar in his church. As he kneeled before the vision, the Virgin placed a priest's robe about his shoulders.

Like many other artists who had tried this subject, Velazquez failed to make a pleasing composition. His picture showed the saint crouching under a tent-like robe, while the Virgin and angels were crowded in the space above. But as Velazquez painted he realized how much he had learned from the Venetian masters' pictures. He was using a freer brush stroke which made the clouds look luminous and the draperies soft and flowing.

In the spring of 1623 Prime Minister Olivares summoned Velazquez to Madrid. Olivares, a native of Seville, had been tutor to Prince Philip. When the sixteen-year-old Prince inherited the throne of Spain, his tutor became Prime Minister and the real ruler of the country. He had known Pacheco in Seville and had seen some of Velazquez' paintings. Impressed by the artist's talent he asked Fonseca to summon the young painter to the court. Fonseca sent Velazquez money for the trip and invited him and Pacheco to visit him in Madrid.

In August, Velazquez, his assistant Pareja, and his father-in-law moved into lodgings provided by Fonseca. A few days later Diego set up an easel and painted a portrait of his host.

ST. ILDEFONSO RECEIVING THE CHASUBLE
About 1625 (64 15/16″ x 55 1/8″)
Archbishop's Palace, Seville

When Fonseca's portrait was shown at court, King and courtiers were enthusiastic. Olivares immediately commissioned Velazquez to paint a portrait of the king. Diego studied the face he was to portray so many times. He was impressed by the dignity of this eighteen-year-old monarch who never showed anger and seldom smiled.

King Philip IV was far from handsome. He had inherited his father's long projecting jaw, thick lower lip, and heavy eyes. But the tall blond king looked distinguished in his plain black clothes.

Never before had an artist painted a truthful likeness of the king, said Olivares when he saw Velazquez' portrait of King Philip. The artist was appointed "Painter to the King," and ordered to bring his family to Madrid.

In October, Velazquez, his wife, and two small daughters moved into an apartment given them by King Philip.

Velazquez set to work on a full-length portrait of the king placing him against a plain gray background. Standing beside a table, Philip held a piece of paper in one hand. His other hand rested on his sword. His stance was restrained but self-assured, his appearance kingly but not pompous. The only notes of color in the picture were the red tablecloth and Philip's full scarlet lips, and the only adornments on the king's black costume were the gold chain across his chest and the stiff white collar at his neck. By the king's command elaborate fashions had been forbidden at the court. Instead of starched lace ruffs, courtiers now wore the plain white collars chosen by the king.

That same year Velazquez painted the king on horseback, "A portrait of King Philip," wrote Pacheco, "armed and on horseback with a baton in his right hand."

At Velazquez' request the painting was shown outside the church of San Felipe. People walking through the main street of Madrid stopped to admire the likeness to the king, "all done from nature," wrote Pacheco, "including the landscape in the background."

PHILIP IV
  1624 (78 3/4″ x 40 1/2″)
  The Metropolitan Museum of Art, New York
  Bequest of Benjamin Altman

Prime Minister Olivares was also Royal Master of the Horse. Velazquez painted him with a whip in one hand and his other hand resting on his sword. He, like the king, wore a gold chain across his chest. A gold bow was pinned on the front of his dark green doublet, and a dark green cape fell from his right shoulder. His nose was long, his mouth, almost hidden by an enormous twirled moustache, was firm, and his dark eyes looked out intelligently from under heavy eyebrows.

This was the man who had seized the reins of government from a king who was too weak to rule. Olivares encouraged Philip's weaknesses. He arranged hunting parties for the king who was an enthusiastic sportsman, and planned entertainments which kept Philip away from affairs of state. Philip was delighted when Olivares provided a studio for Velazquez in the royal palace, for he loved to watch the artist paint. He felt at ease with the quiet painter, six years older than himself. Other artists were jealous of Velazquez, whose portraits were so popular at the court. They told the king that Velazquez could paint only portraits, which were the lowest form of art. Velazquez was unconcerned:

"These gentlemen pay me a great compliment," he replied, knowing that his portraits were better than any other artist's.

But Philip was so anxious to prove Velazquez' talent, that he proposed a painting competition. The subject was the expulsion of the Moors from Spain. Philip was not surprised when Velazquez' painting won the prize. It showed King Philip's father dressed in armor pointing to a crowd of weeping Moors who were led in chains by Spanish soldiers. In the distance were the ships which would carry away the prisoners. On the right a woman in armor represented Spain.

Philip rewarded his favorite artist by appointing him "Gentleman Usher" in charge of the lighting, heating, and rooming accommodations at the palace. Twenty-eight-year-old Velazquez accepted the title gratefully, as few artists had been honored at so young an age, but he soon realized that his duties as an usher would make him a prisoner at the court.

COUNT-DUKE OLIVARES
1624 (87 5/8″ x 53 15/16″)
Hispanic Society of America, New York

In the fall of 1628 Peter Paul Rubens arrived at court. Velazquez had heard a great deal about this handsome, courtly painter who was also an ambassador from his country. This time the artist came from Flanders to persuade King Philip to make peace with England.

Olivares provided Rubens with a studio, so that before he returned to Flanders he could paint portraits of the royal family. Velazquez, watching the older painter working, marvelled at his boldness, skill, and speed. He was pleased when the Flemish artist praised his modest portraits of the king, which, unlike Rubens' glowing portraits did not glorify the sitter.

The artists visited the Escorial one day to study the paintings by Italian masters. Rubens, who had once lived in Italy, urged Velazquez to visit the country where these artists had lived and worked. He would learn how the masters composed pictures filled with many figures and how they achieved an effect of atmosphere and depth.

These were problems Velazquez could not solve in a picture he was painting for the king. It showed Bacchus, god of wine, surrounded by a group of drinking peasants. The drinkers looked like the Spanish peasants Velazquez had painted in his *bodegones*. Each face was a lively study in itself, but the half-nude Bacchus whose smooth white skin contrasted with the swarthy complexions of the peasants had little relation to the other figures.

The scene, which was supposed to be outdoors, was painted by a studio light coming from the left, so that the figures crowded in the foregound seemed to be set against, not in, the landscape.

Many months passed before the king allowed his favorite painter to go to Italy. Finally, Velazquez received permission to leave Madrid. Olivares made arrangements for the trip. The artist was given money and letters of introduction. He would travel by ship under the protection of General Spinola, commander of the Spanish troops in Italy. In August, 1629, Velazquez and his assistant arrived in Barcelona where they boarded the general's ship. A few days later they set sail for Genoa.

THE DRINKERS (Los Borrachos)
1628 (65″ x 88 5/8″)
Prado, Madrid

Velazquez left Spinola at Milan, and continued on to Venice, the glittering island city where Titian had lived and worked. The Spanish ambassador gave him lodgings and an escort to show him about the city. He studied Titian's paintings and copied pictures by Tintoretto, another great Venetian master. He noted how the artist composed groups of figures, and how he painted dazzling effects of light.

A few weeks later Velazquez headed south. The trip to Rome was long, but he was greeted cordially in the cities where he stopped. The Cardinal of Ferrara invited him to visit in his palace. When Velazquez refused because, like other Spaniards, he preferred to eat dinner very late, the Cardinal offered him a house and provided him with food. In Rome he was given lodging in the Vatican and permission to copy Michelangelo's paintings in the Pope's private chapel. But Velazquez found the Pope's palace inconvenient. When summer came he asked for a room in the Duke of Medici's villa on a hill which overlooked the city. He sketched antique statues in the garden and studied the Roman paintings in the villa. These ancient pictures inspired him to illustrate a Roman myth.

Velazquez' painting showed Apollo, god of light, visiting the forge of Vulcan. The god of fire listened horrified as Apollo told him that Vulcan's beloved Venus had been unfaithful. The swarthy, bearded blacksmith looked like the peasants in Velazquez' painting of "The Drinkers," but these figures were not crowded in the foreground. For the first time Velazquez had flooded his picture with a soft warm light which gave an effect of depth and unity to the scene.

In the fall Velazquez caught a fever. The Spanish ambassador, fearing for the painter's life, brought the invalid to his house and provided him with medicines and special foods. Velazquez was soon well enough to go to Naples where he painted a portrait of King Philip's sister. There he received an urgent message from the king. Velazquez must hurry home at once in order to paint a portrait of King Philip's baby son.

THE FORGE OF VULCAN
1630 (87 3/4" x 114")
Prado, Madrid

When Velazquez arrived at court he was ordered by Olivares to present himself to the king. During the year and a half that Velazquez had been absent Philip had not allowed himself to be painted by any other artist. Now he was waiting anxiously for his favorite artist to paint a portrait of the little prince.

A faint smile lighted up King Philip's face as Velazquez kneeled and kissed his hand. He was eager for the painter to see his son who was learning how to walk.

Velazquez watched fascinated as the prince's favorite dwarf led the little boy around the room. The dark ugliness of the dwarf contrasted sharply with the blond beauty of the child. Prince Baltasar Carlos had inherited his mother's delicate face and alert expression instead of his father's heavy jaw and melancholy eyes. The sight of the dwarf leading the little prince made a deep impression on Velazquez who decided to make it the subject of a picture.

He placed the dwarf in the foreground of the picture, and the prince behind him on a higher level. In this way Velazquez showed that the monarch was superior to his servant. The dwarf's face was partly hidden in deep shadow. In one hand he held an apple and in the other a rattle designed to look like a royal scepter. His head was turned in the direction of the prince as he gave the signal to walk forward.

The prince grasped a baton firmly in one hand. His other hand rested on his sword. He wore a gold-embroidered dress over an armored vest, and a purple sash across his chest. His black plumed hat had been placed on a purple cushion at his left. A strong light played directly on his childish face, making him the center of the picture. This alert, handsome child, who moved forward with a determined step, was every inch a prince.

PRINCE BALTASAR CARLOS AND HIS DWARF
1631 (53 1/2″ x 41″)
Museum of Fine Arts, Boston

"When Velazquez painted the king on horseback," wrote Pacheco, "he had him seated for three hours at a time."

Philip who was one of the best riders in the country sat astride a rearing chestnut horse. He wore black armor etched with gold, and a purple sash across his chest. His big black hat trimmed with rose-colored plumes contrasted with his blond complexion. His twirled moustache and short pointed beard, which he had grown while Velazquez was away, made him look older and more self-assured. Sitting erect with reins in one hand and a baton in the other he appeared to be a forceful monarch.

For the first time Velazquez placed his model against a landscape background so that the horse and rider were sharply outlined against distant snow-capped mountains and a cloudy sky.

This was one of the portraits Velazquez painted for the country palace which Olivares was building for the King. While masons and carpenters worked frantically to finish the palace for the formal presentation, Velazquez and assistants were painting portraits of the royal family to decorate the "Hall of Realms."

PHILIP IV
About 1634 (118 3/4″ x 123 7/8″)
Prado, Madrid

Compared to Velazquez' spirited picture of the king, the portrait of the queen, painted by a less skilled artist, looked stiff and lifeless. Velazquez hastily retouched the horse's head and repainted the queen's lovely face.

The royal portraits were still unfinished when Olivares decided to present the Buen Retiro palace to the king. On the first of December, 1633, Philip and Olivares fought a tournament in the palace courtyard, and in the evening a pageant was presented in the brightly lighted garden.

Velazquez, who was in charge of the festivities, had little time to enjoy the celebrations. He painted every day till sundown and every evening he performed his duties for the court. Burdened by his extra work Velazquez asked the king to transfer his title of Usher to his young assistant Mazo. In 1634, Juan Bautista Mazo, now married to Velazquez' oldest daughter, became Gentleman Usher of the court, and Velazquez set to work finishing the portraits of the royal family.

The next year the Hall of Realms was opened. The portraits of the king and queen were hanging at the entrance end. Queen Isabel on a white horse faced her husband on a chestnut charger, and just above the doorway which separated the pictures of the monarchs was a portrait of the little prince astride a cantering pony.

QUEEN ISABEL OF BOURBON
About 1634 (118″ x 123 3/4″)
Prado, Madrid

Prince Baltasar Carlos was a fearless rider. The king and queen loved to watch him galloping around the ring while Olivares, standing in the center cracked his whip with each command. His little legs reached only halfway down his pony's bulging flanks, but his feet were firmly planted in his stirrups, his back was erect and his reins held high.

Velazquez' portrait showed the five-year-old prince wearing a big black hat like his father's. He, too, wore a purple sash across his chest and held a baton in his hand. Prince Baltasar Carlos astride his chestnut pony looked like a little king.

Velazquez brushed in his paint so thinly that the shadows seemed more transparent and the lights more radiant than they had in the portrait of the king. This picture of a horse and rider cantering across the slopes outside Madrid was bathed in fresh outdoor light. For the first time Velazquez had shown his model in, not against, a landscape setting.

PRINCE BALTASAR CARLOS
About 1634 (82 1/4″ x 68″)
Prado, Madrid

While Velazquez was working on the royal portraits other artists were painting events from Spanish history for the Hall of Realms. They were enormous canvases picturing Spanish victories during King Philip's reign. Many were crowded and confused.

One painting by Jose Leonardo pictured the surrender of Breda to the Spaniards. There had been great excitement in Madrid when this city in the Netherlands surrendered to Spinola. Velazquez had often heard the story about the gallant general who did not allow the vanquished governor to kneel when he presented the keys of the city to his conqueror. Then some years later the artist had come to know and like this general who treated his enemies with respect.

When Velazquez saw Leonardo's stilted picture of the Breda surrender, he decided to paint a picture of the scene as he saw it in his mind. In this way he would honor his friend Spinola who had died five years before.

Velazquez placed Spinola and the governor in the center of the canvas. At first he showed the general with his arms about the governor's neck, then decided the gesture looked dramatic. He quickly repainted the figure of Spinola, so that one hand rested on Justin of Nassau's shoulder. The understanding gesture of the general's outstretched arm, the look of compassion on his face, and the grateful expression of the governor told the story of the picture. Spinola's troops were massed behind him, their tall lances pointing to the sky. Some of Justin of Nassau's tired soldiers stood on the other side, and more could be seen marching in the sunlight between the central figures. The faces in the background were brushed in so thinly that they looked like mere impressions, but the faces in the foreground were thickly painted and smoothed over with great care. Although the picture was painted in a studio the scene was flooded with out-door light.

When Velazquez' painting was hung in the Hall of Realms, Leonardo's picture looked flat and lifeless. Without pomp Velazquez had pictured a human story which was a moving tribute to his noble friend.

THE SURRENDER OF BREDA
1634-5 (121″ x 144 1/2″)
Prado, Madrid

Count-Duke Olivares, prime minister of Spain and commander-in-chief of the royal army, had never taken part in any battle, but when he had his portrait painted by Velazquez he asked the artist to picture him as a general. Velazquez painted Olivares wearing black armor, a purple sash, and a big plumed hat. Astride a chestnut charger he waved his general's baton in the direction of the fleeing enemy.

Olivares in his early fifties was the most powerful man in Spain. He also had many bitter enemies. Queen Isabel never forgave him for planning extravagant entertainments for her husband, and statesmen grumbled that he spent government money on the Buen Retiro palace, while the country was at war with France. But Velazquez remained faithful to his friend who had introduced him to the court. When Olivares finally fell from power, Velazquez was the only man who dared to visit the Count-Duke in exile.

Olivares' portrait was the last picture Velazquez painted for the Buen Retiro palace. It was hung in the Hall of Realms with portraits of the royal family and paintings glorifying Spain.

COUNT-DUKE OLIVARES
    About 1635 (123″ x 94″)
    Prado, Madrid

For several years Velazquez had been working on portraits for the royal hunting lodge. The portraits showed members of the Royal Family dressed as hunters. Because he had been constantly interrupted by his duties at Court he was still working on the portrait of King Philip's brother, although his model was no longer in Madrid.

Prince Cardinal Fernando, Governor of the Netherlands had his brother's heavy jaw and full projecting lower lip. He wore high boots, a dark suit with embroidered sleeves, yellow gauntlets, and a dark peaked cap. Gun in hand he stood beside his dog against a background of sky and mountains.

Using small rapid brush strokes Velazquez painted the dog's glistening coat. The quivering hound looked very much alive. Using broader strokes he brushed in feathery dark green foliage on the right, and in the background he painted a gray-green slope spattered with yellow sunlight, a distant blue mountain, and a luminous gray-blue sky.

PRINCE CARDINAL FERNANDO IN HUNTING DRESS
1632-5 (75 1/4″ x 42 1/8″)
Prado, Madrid

In 1635 when Philip's brother-in-law became king of Hungary, the king asked Velazquez to plan an elaborate celebration at the Buen Retiro palace. Velazquez hired landscape gardeners who constructed ponds, canals, and grottos in the park. He supervised the building of an open-air theater in the garden, and imported Italian artists to design the settings.

One spring evening lords and ladies dressed in shimmering silks and sparkling jewels took their places in the double row of balconies surrounding a brightly lighted stage. They sat spellbound watching earthquakes, shipwrecks, and cupids flying through the air.

Velazquez was given little credit for the job, although it had kept him from his painting. Whenever he found time he worked on a portrait of the prince for the hunting lodge. The prince, like his father, was an enthusiastic hunter. Courtiers cringed when six-year-old Baltasar Carlos armed with a small size gun accompanied the king on hunting parties, but the prince was as skilled a marksman as many of the guests. When he posed for Velazquez he planted his feet firmly on the ground and grasped his gun securely in his hand. His costume was like his uncle's except for the lace collar at his neck. His dark cap, tilted jauntily on his head, framed his blond hair and childlike face. A fat dog slept at his feet and an alert hound sat on the other side. In the background were the blue-green Guadarrama mountains just outside Madrid.

In 1636 the picture was ready for the hunting lodge, but the prince's portrait did not fit the panel where it was supposed to hang. Velazquez hastily cut a strip from the right edge of the canvas, so that only the head and paws of the hound were showing in the picture.

PRINCE BALTASAR CARLOS IN HUNTING DRESS
1635
Prado, Madrid

At the king's request Velazquez painted two more pictures for the hunting lodge. The tall narrow canvases pictured two strange figures which were different from any Velazquez had painted at the court. The ragged characters, named for ancient Greek philosophers looked like the peasants in Velazquez' *bodegones*, but unlike his early paintings the figures were bathed in soft transparent light.

It was a relief to paint these rough-hewn models, after years of working on portraits of the royal family. Using long-handled brushes he slashed on paint in broad rapid strokes, sometimes so thinly that the canvas showed and sometimes thickly to give a surface texture.

Velazquez showed Aesop, author of the famous fables, holding a book in one hand; the other hand was thrust in the fold of his shabby brown robe. The philosopher's lower lip was thrust forward and his droopy eyes were thoughtful as if he were about to comment on the foolishness of mankind.

Menippus, the cynic, huddled in his dark gray cloak, looked suspiciously over his shoulder. His eyes were watchful, his mouth drawn down as if he distrusted all mankind.

AESOP
About 1639 (70 1/2″ x 37″)
Prado, Madrid

MENIPPUS
About 1639 (70 1/2″ x 37″)
Prado, Madrid

One night in 1643 a sealed coach accompanied by four terrified horsemen secretly left Madrid. The next day people learned that Prime Minister Olivares had been banished.

King Philip suddenly took over the responsibilities of his government. Early in 1644 he decided to visit the battlefront where the war with the French was going badly. He was accompanied by Velazquez and a train of servants, dwarfs, and courtiers.

"I have returned to this kingdom," he wrote a friend from Aragon, "leaving behind the companionship of the Queen and my children and the conveniences of my house."

All through the frigid winter Philip toured the battlefront. His tired soldiers cheered when he appeared before them wearing the red and silver uniform of the Spanish army.

Three times Philip posed for Velazquez in a drafty shack. Although he grasped his general's baton with assurance the king looked old and weary. His hair was limp, his eyes droopy, and his jaw heavier than before.

Velazquez brushed in the monarch's face as quickly as he could, modeling the features in subtle flesh tones. With rapid flecks of gray and white he captured the effect of sparkling silver trimming on the king's scarlet coat.

Philip's presence at the front restored the confidence of his soldiers. Suddenly the tide of battle turned. In August the Spaniards won a smashing victory at Lerida. A few days later the grateful citizens staged a triumphal entry for their king. At their request, Velazquez' portrait of the king was hung in the church under a canopy of embroidered gold. All day people filed by the picture, marvelling at the glowing red and shimmering silver of the monarch's uniform and the expression of kingly dignity on his tired, unhandsome face.

Before King Philip left Lerida he ordered Velazquez to ship his portait to Madrid, so that the Queen could see him wearing the uniform of the Spanish army. In the same crate, Velazquez packed another picture. This was a portrait of Philip's favorite dwarf, who was also secretary to the king.

PHILIP IV
1644 (51 1/8″ x 39 1/8″)
Frick Collection, New York

Philip loved to surround himself with dwarfs. It amused him to see them dressed as courtiers running awkwardly on their stunted legs, and their acid wit sometimes made him smile. He never travelled without his favorite dwarf "El Primo," who was in charge of official documents at the court.

Don Diego de Acedo, nicknamed "El Primo" (cousin) because he was of noble birth, was a man of great intelligence who had accepted his deformity with poise. When Velazquez painted El Primo's portrait he did not disguise the dwarf's ill-proportioned body. He showed him dressed in black seated on a rock. An inkwell and notebooks rested on the ground beside him. His little hands turned the pages of an enormous book which he balanced on his outstretched leg. The other short leg barely touched the ground. His tragic face, framed by a big black hat, was that of a man who had suffered with great dignity.

DON DIEGO DE ACEDO—"EL PRIMO"
  1644 (41 1/8″ x 32 1/4″)
  Prado, Madrid

Soon after Philip returned to court Queen Isabel of Bourbon died. Although he never allowed himself to show his grief the king was deeply saddened by the loss. Without the queen, life in Madrid seemed sad and lonely. In the spring of 1646 Philip decided to tour the battlefront again. With him went Velazquez, a train of dwarfs and courtiers and the king's sixteen-year-old son, Prince Baltasar Carlos.

It was a tiring trip, but in every city people cheered the handsome prince who would some day become king of Spain. The king and his train pushed on from town to town until one day the prince fell ill. While the royal party waited for Baltasar Carlos to recover, Velazquez set up a studio and painted the prince's favorite dwarf.

Sebastian De Morra, dressed in a green doublet and red cloak was seated on the ground, his short legs sticking straight in front of him, his hands thrust menacingly in his belt. With rapid brush strokes Velazquez captured the intense look in the dwarf's smoldering eyes.

In the summer the royal party arrived in Zaragossa where the prince announced his engagement to his cousin, thirteen-year-old Princess Mariana. Citizens and courtiers celebrated madly, but Philip worried that his son looked pale and thin. In October Baltasar caught a chill. A few weeks later he was dead.

"Mine is such grief as you can conceive at such a loss," wrote Philip to a friend, then added, "I am full of resignation."

A sad and lonely king returned to Madrid that fall. The heads of state conferred and agreed that Philip should marry the princess who had been chosen for his son.

Forty-three-year-old Philip waited impatiently for his niece Mariana to arrive from Austria. This bride-to-be, only two years older than his daughter, would bring gaiety to the court.

While Philip waited he ordered Velazquez to redecorate the gloomy palace. Velazquez welcomed the job, hoping that the king would send him to Italy to buy paintings. In January,1649, Philip reluctantly permitted the painter to leave Madrid. A few weeks later, Velazquez and his assistant arrived in Venice.

DON SEBASTIAN DE MORRA
About 1645 (41 3/4″ x 31 7/8″)
Prado, Madrid

Venice gave Velazquez an enthusiastic welcome.

"A cavalier breathing as great dignity
    As any other person in authority,"

wrote a Venetian poet about the famous artist.

Velazquez bought a few glowing canvases by Venetian masters, then headed south for Rome.

Twenty years had passed since he had visited the Holy City. Then he had been an unknown artist, but now he was one of Europe's greatest painters and an ambassador from the king of Spain. He was welcomed cordially by cardinals and princes and by well-known artists who helped him select pieces of sculpture for King Philip's palace. He spent many hours painting portraits, but in between commissions he found time to visit the Medici Villa where he had spent one happy summer. As he strolled through the shady gardens he noted the changing lights at different times of day. One afternoon he painted a boarded-up archway topped by a marble balustrade. Above were dark green cypresses silhouetted against a pale blue sky.

One sunny morning he painted another archway with a statue and cypresses in the background. He brushed on the paint thinly, leaving parts of the white canvas showing, so that the picture seemed to be flooded with transparent light. With quick nervous strokes he captured the effect of sunlight flickering through the trees. This lightly painted sketch was a lively study of shimmering light and shade.

From Madrid came letters from the king urging Velazquez to hurry home.

"Since you know his phlegmatic temperament," Philip wrote to the Spanish ambassador in Rome, ". . . it would be well that he hasten the conclusion of the work."

Velazquez had little desire to return to his duties at the court. Ignoring the king's impatient letters he lingered on in Rome.

VIEW OF GARDEN OF VILLA MEDICI, ROME. "NOON"
    1650 (17 3/4″ x 15″)
    Prado, Madrid

VIEW OF GARDEN OF VILLA MEDICI, ROME. "EVENING"
    1650 (19″ x 16 1/2″)
    Prado, Madrid

Velazquez reported to the king that the copies of antique statues which he had ordered for the palace were still unfinished. While he waited he painted portraits of artists, cardinals and princes. The Pope, impressed by the artist's speed and skill commissioned a portrait of himself. This was the most important order Velazquez had received in Rome, and he wondered if, in a few sittings, he could paint a portrait which would please the Pope.

Before he undertook the task he decided to try his hand at one more portrait. His assistant, Juan de Pareja, was glad to be Velazquez' model. He wore a green doublet with dark green sleeves. His white lace collar contrasted with his dark complexion. Velazquez painted as quickly as he could, brushing in the Moor's black bushy hair, his fuzzy mustache and beard, and his dark shiny eyes which looked out proudly from the canvas.

When Velazquez exhibited the portrait at the Pantheon, it attracted more attention than any other painting. A few days later he was made a member of the artists' guild, an honor seldom awarded to a Spanish painter.

Encouraged by this tribute, Velazquez set to work painting a portrait of the Pope.

JUAN DE PAREJA
  1650 (29 15/16″ x 25 3/16″)
  Longford Castle, England
  Collection Earl of Radnor

Pope Innocent X was so ugly that many cardinals had opposed his election to the papal throne. In a few short sittings Velazquez painted the Pope's coarse greasy face which was almost as red as his cap and cape, and the velvet chair and curtain in the background. With quick slippery strokes he painted the Pope's shimmering satin cape so that the brilliant costume outshone the frightening redness of the pontiff's face. Only the Pope's white collar and surplice relieved the garish redness of the picture. So skillfully did Velazquez capture the suspicious expression in his sitter's blue-gray eyes that the Pope exclaimed "Too true! too true!" when he saw the finished portrait.

Velazquez knew that this was the best portrait he had painted since he had been in Rome. He proudly signed his name on the piece of paper which the Pope was holding, and, for the first time, he made a copy of his painting which he planned to take to Spain.

Velazquez was still not ready to leave the Holy City, for members of the Pope's household clamored to have their portraits painted by the Spanish artist. The Pope's sister-in-law, barber, head steward, and master of the bed chamber all had their portraits painted by Velazquez.

Philip continued to send messages from Madrid urging Velazquez to return so that he could paint a portrait of his young bride, who had just arrived from Austria. He sent the artist money for the journey, ordering him to come by sea, not land, so that he would not be tempted to linger on the way. Velazquez could no longer make excuses to the king. Now that his mission for Philip was completed he knew it was time for him to leave the city where he had enjoyed two years of freedom.

In June, 1651, Velazquez arrived in Spain and became once more a prisoner of the king.

POPE INNOCENT X
1650 (55 1/4″ x 57 1/4″)
Doria Gallery, Rome

Soon after Velazquez arrived at court the queen's first child, a little girl, was born. For some weeks Queen Mariana did not feel well enough to have her portrait painted, so Velazquez had time to install the paintings and statues he had brought from Italy. Soon the dark palace rooms began to look more cheerful. A few months later Velazquez was appointed Palace Marshal. He was given a four-floor apartment, library, and storeroom in the palace, but in return he had to perform extra duties at the court. Whenever the king and his court moved to the Escorial or some other summer palace, Velazquez organized the transportation. He was away from his apartment for several months each year, and during these months he had little time to paint.

In between these tiring trips Velazquez painted portraits of the royal family. The seventeen-year-old queen posed for the artist many times. Velazquez wondered why King Philip was so enchanted by his homely little wife, who had inherited his family's heavy jaw and dull lifeless eyes. She was a stupid girl who laughed uproariously at the clowning of the dwarfs and loved to frighten her ladies-in-waiting by releasing mice from under her wide skirts. While Philip went hunting, she played happily with her husband's daughter, two years younger than herself.

Velazquez was appalled by the grotesque appearance of the queen encased in a tight black bodice trimmed with silver, and a wide, tent-like skirt. Her sullen face, heavily rouged, was dwarfed by an enormous wig trimmed with ornaments and plumes. Velazquez painted her as she was, then skillfully added brilliant spots of color. Her scarlet lips and large blue eyes, and the bright red ribbons at her wrists helped to relieve the somber atmosphere of the picture.

MARIANA OF AUSTRIA, QUEEN OF SPAIN
1652-3 (82 1/4″ x 49″)
Prado, Madrid

Princess Maria Theresa, Philip's oldest daughter, was far more intelligent than her playmate, Queen Mariana.

For some time Philip had been hoping to find the suitable husband for his charming daughter. He commissioned Velazquez to paint portraits of the princess to send to every court in Europe. The Duke of Flanders, the Emperor of Germany, and the King of France all received pictures of the Spanish princess.

In a portrait which Velazquez painted for the Austrian Emperor, the fourteen-year-old princess was dressed according to the absurd fashion popular at the court. Her white dress with tight bodice and wide skirt was trimmed with rose and silver. Two watches were suspended by pink ribbons from her waist, and in one hand she held a white handkerchief trimmed with lace. Her cheeks were coated with brilliant rouge and her blond hair hidden by a monstrous wig decorated with plumes, rosettes, and ribbons.

PRINCESS MARIA THERESA
1652-3 (50 3/8″ x 38 9/16″)
Kunsthistorisches Museum, Vienna

Philip at forty-eight looked old and sad. He had aged greatly since Velazquez had painted him in his red and silver uniform. During the past ten years he had been burdened by affairs of state and saddened by the loss of his first wife and only son. Although he delighted in his young bride and baby daughter he longed for a son who would inherit the throne of Spain.

"Oh, Sor Maria," he exclaimed one day, "what grievous blows our Lord has given me!"

Velazquez painted the aging monarch with sympathy and understanding. Although his hair was limp, his jaw heavy and his pale blue eyes were dull, there was an expression of kingly dignity in Philip's sad tired face.

PHILIP IV
1653 (27 3/16″ x 22 1/16″)
Prado, Madrid

Philip's youngest daughter, Margarita, was the darling of the court. The fair-haired princess looked like a little doll dressed in long dresses covered with bows, ornaments, and lace. When she was three her ladies-in-waiting brought her to Velazquez' studio to have her portrait painted. While her attendants posed her with one hand resting on a table and arranged the ruffles of her dress, Velazquez had time to study the child's solemn face. He knew he must paint quickly before the princess grew too restless. In a few hours he captured the soft radiance of Margarita's golden hair and the delicate flesh tones of her face. After the child had left he brushed in her rose and silver ruffled dress, a bunch of flowers on the table, and a blue-green curtain in the background.

Velazquez painted many portraits of the princess which were sent to every court in Europe. Each year she was a little taller and her blond hair was longer, but in every picture she wore the grotesque dresses which were fashionable at court.

Velazquez felt sorry for his little model who posed so stiffly for her portrait. Then one day when he was painting a portrait of the princess, Margarita suddenly announced that she did not want to pose. In this fleeting moment Velazquez saw the princess as she really was, a lively, willful child who had always been the center of attention. The scene remained so vivid in his mind that he decided to make it a subject of a painting.

PRINCESS MARGARITA
1653-54 (50 1/2″ x 39 1/2″)
Kunsthistorisches Museum, Vienna

Sunlight streaming through a window of Velazquez' dark lofty studio shone on the radiant figure of the little princess, who had just announced that she didn't want to pose. She wore a dress of shimmering white silk and her delicate face was framed by soft golden hair. She paid no attention to the lady-in-waiting who knelt beside her. Her questioning gaze was fixed on the king and queen who were standing outside the picture but whose faces were reflected in the mirror just above the princess's head. On the left, in the darkest corner of the studio, stood Velazquez by his easel. His bronzed face and bushy black hair were barely visible against the shadowy background. He too seemed to be looking at the king and queen.

Half sunlight coming from windows on the right played here and there on the other figures in the room. It glanced across the face of the lady-in-waiting on the princess's left, and picked out the misshapen features of the girl dwarf who was dressed in green velvet trimmed with silver. Beside the dwarf was a little boy in red who rested one foot on the back of a big dog which was sleeping in the foreground. A nun and a courtier, standing behind the other figures were partly hidden in deep shadow.

At the far end of the deep lofty room a man in black stood silhouetted in a sunlit doorway. This gentleman, Don Jose Velazquez was Diego's cousin and director of the royal tapestry factory in Madrid.

Philip loved to watch Velazquez working on this picture, so different from any he had ever seen. Never before had a Spanish artist recorded an informal moment in court life, and never before had Velazquez included a portrait of himself in a picture of the royal family.

When Velazquez was made a knight of Santiago two years later, Philip asked the artist to make one addition to his painting. Following the king's directions, Velazquez picked up a brush and painted the red cross of Santiago on the front of his black velvet doublet.

[64]

THE MAIDS OF HONOR (Las Meninas)
1656 (125″ x 118 1/2″)
Prado, Madrid

Velazquez often visited the royal tapestry factory to consult the director, Jose Velazquez, about hangings for the palace. One day while he was talking with his cousin he noticed three ladies examining a tapestry which they planned to buy. Suddenly an idea for a painting flashed across his mind.

In the shadowy foreground Velazquez placed a group of women weavers. One, in a white blouse, was winding yarn, another was carding wool while a cat played with the wads of yarn lying at her feet. An old woman with a white scarf about her head was sitting at her spinning wheel. She looked towards the girl beside her who drew aside a curtain revealing a sunlit alcove in the background.

Three ladies standing just inside the entrance to the alcove seemed to be spectators at a play about the goddess Pallas and the Greek girl Arachne. The armored goddess, arm upraised was about to turn Arachne into a spider, because she had made a tapestry more beautiful than any woven by a goddess. The backdrop for this scene was a tapestry which pictured another tale from Greek mythology. This hanging, designed by Titian and woven in the royal factory seemed to link the workers in the foreground with the alcove in the background.

Philip often studied this perplexing painting which told two stories on one canvas. He marvelled at Velazquez' skillful use of light and shade which combined the tapestry workers in the foreground with a scene from Greek mythology in the background.

In November, 1659, Philip awarded the cross of Santiago to his favorite painter. Never before had Spain's highest order been given to a man of humble birth who had earned a living by his hands. At the same time the king cancelled the artist's salary to prove that Velazquez, now a noble, received no money for his work. In this way Philip rewarded his favorite painter for thirty-six years of faithful service.

THE TAPESTRY WEAVERS
1657 (86 1/2″ x 113 1/2″)
Prado, Madrid

There was great rejoicing at the court when Philip's son and heir was born. He was only two when the king commissioned Velazquez to paint his portrait. The pale, fair-haired prince wore a white apron over a rose dress trimmed with silver. The claw, the bell, and the perfumed ball hanging from his belt were supposed to guard him from disease. He paid no attention to the puppy squirming in the chair beside him. The sickly prince did not live to inherit the throne. Two years after he had his portrait painted, Prince Philip Prosper died.

In the spring of 1660 Philip asked his Palace Marshal to plan the wedding of Princess Maria Theresa to King Louis XIV of France. The marriage which marked the end of Spain's long war with France would take place on a little island in the river which divided the two countries.

Velazquez hurried to the Isle of Pheasants to plan the building of a pavilion and to arrange accommodations for the court. While Philip, his daughter, and hundreds of courtiers progressed slowly northward, King Louis and his flashy train were moving south from Paris.

On the fourth of June the royal parties met in the pavilion on the Isle of Pheasants, where Philip presented his pretty daughter to the handsome king of France. Velazquez dressed as a knight of Santiago handed King Philip's presents to the bridegroom. A few days later the Palace Marshal, too tired to enjoy the festivities he had planned, headed for Madrid.

All through the summer Velazquez, exhausted from overwork, continued to perform his duties at the court, until one day he fell ill. Even the king's doctor could not cure his fever. On the sixth of August King Philip's friend and favorite painter died.

"I am overwhelmed," wrote Philip when he learned the news.

Velazquez' body in the uniform of a knight of Santiago was taken to the church of St. John the Baptist. The next day artists, statesmen, and courtiers paid their respects. They did not know that this unassuming artist would live forever in his paintings of peasants, poets, and statesmen, of generals, Popes, and dwarfs, and in his truthful but understanding portraits of the Spanish royal family.

PRINCE PHILIP PROSPER
1659 (50 1/2″ x 39″)
Kunsthistorisches Museum, Vienna

BIBLIOGRAPHY

Aman, Jean Edmond Francois. *Velazquez*. Felix Alcani, Paris, 1913.

Armstrong, Sir Walter. *The Life of Velazquez*. Seeley & Co. Ltd. The Macmillan Co., New York, 1896.

Balry, Alfred Lye. *Velazquez*. George Newnes Ltd., London.

Bensusan, Susan Levy. *Velazquez*. T. C. & E. C. Jack, London. F. A. Stokes, New York, 1907.

Beruete, y Monet, Aureliano de. *Velazquez in Prado Museum*. 1914.

————. *Velazquez*. Methuen & Co., London, 1906.

Borelius, Leon. *Etudes sur Velazquez*. P. A. Norstedt, 1949.

Bréal, Auguste. *Velazquez*. G. Cres, Paris, 1919.

Calvert, Albert Frederick. *Velazquez*. John Lane, London, 1908.

Fargue, Leon Paul. *Velazquez*. Divan, Paris, 1946.

Faure, Elie. *Velazquez*. H. Laurens, Paris, 1904.

Grappe, Georges. *Velazquez*. Plon, Paris, 1940.

Justi, Karl D. *Velazquez and His Times*. H. Grevel & Co., London, 1889.

Lafort, Paul. *Velazquez*. Librairie de l'art, Paris, 1888.

La Fuente, Ferrari, Enrique. *Velazquez*. Translated by James Emmons from the French version of the original Spanish. Skira. Distributed by World Publishing Co. Cleveland, 1960.

————. *The Paintings and Drawings of Velazquez*. Phaidon Press, London. Oxford University Press, New York, 1943.

Lopez-Rey, José. *Velazquez*. Catalogue Raisoné. Faber and Faber, London, 1963.

Mayer, August L. *Velazquez*. Catalogue Raisoné of the pictures and drawings. Faber & Faber, London, 1936.

————. *Velazquez*. Editions Pierre Tisné, Paris, (c. 1940.)

Pantarbia, Bernadino de. *La Vida y la Obra de Velazquez*. Campania Bibliografia Espanola, S. H., Madrid, 1955.

Riggs, A. Stanley. *Velazquez, Painter of Truth and Prisoner of the King*. Bobbs Merrill, New York, 1946.

Salas, Xavier de. *Velazquez*. Phaidon Publishers, Inc. Distributed by New York Graphic Society Publishers, Ltd., Greenwich, Conn., 1962.

Stevenson, Robert A. M. *Velazquez*. G. Bell & Sons Ltd., London, 1962.

Stirling-Maxwell, Sir William. *Velazquez and His Works*. J. W. Parker & Son, London, 1855.

Trapier, Elizabeth du Gué. *Velazquez*. Printed by order of the Trustees Hispanic Society, New York, 1948.

Velazquez, Introduction by José Ortega y Gasset. Phaidon House, Inc., New York, 1953.

INDEX